Introduction

Social studies projects and research activities are a great way to provide students with some of their most valuable learning experiences based on cultural, historical, community-oriented, and global topics. Research requires that students become active learners. It requires them to think and to act upon their thinking.

When they hear the word "research", students often envision long hours of boring work. Perhaps you envision long hours of tedious preparation and grading. However, this book of projects and research activities has been designed to make research an exciting means by which students can be involved in their own learning. The featured activities and projects are also simple and easy to implement and evaluate for teachers.

Developing cognitive and higher order reasoning skills are important goals most teachers have for their students. This book is the perfect way for teachers to achieve these goals while incorporating some valuable social studies concepts at the same time.

Each social studies project or research activity featured includes teacher instructions, a reproducible student page explaining the project, and a grade sheet to simplify and encourage objectivity in grading.

Some of the projects have been designed specifically as group projects. Others can easily be adapted to incorporate cooperative methods. Still others involve individual participation. Regardless of how you choose to implement them in your classroom, your work load will be lighter and your expectations clear as students progress through some very challenging and relevant activities.

Before you begin each project, read through the teacher and student instructions and familiarize yourself with the grade sheet(s) as well. It is also advisable to show and explain to students the grade sheet(s) when you assign a project. This allows them to understand exactly how their work will be evaluated before they start.

Finally! A book filled with meaningful social studies research projects and activities for students—and an easy means to implement and evaluate them! Research has never been more stimulating, rewarding, or simple.

Teacher Instructions

Biographical Sketch

Whether you are studying economics, ancient world history, your own state, or a unit on civil rights, this is an excellent activity for introducing students to people who have shaped the lives of many. This is also a good "beginning" project you can use to expose your students to initial research.

appropriate subjects for use: all social studies
critical thinking skills developed: knowledge, comprehension

Give your students a list of names related to your topic of study, or assign a particular name to each student. The student will research and write a three-paragraph biography on the person.

Hint # 1: This is a great activity to use during Black History Month. Assign students the names of lesser known African Americans.

Hint # 2: Use this project to introduce your students to musicians, artists, writers, composers, and actors of the time frame you are studying.

Hint # 3: Go to the library as a class. You can help students find sources and keep them away from the encyclopedias. *Current Biographies* is a good source you might want them to use.

Hint # 4: To increase oral communication skills, biographical sketches can also be presented to and shared with the class.

Name _____ Date _____

Student Instructions

Biographical Sketch

Due Date: _____

You are to research and write a three-paragraph biography about _____.
The purpose of this activity is for you to get to know the person about whom you are writing.

Ask yourself these questions:

- *Why is this person important?*
- *What has this person contributed to society?*
- *How did the person's life experiences influence his or her contribution(s)?*

You are required to turn in the following, in this order:

- *grade sheet (with your name on it; see page 4)*
- *finished paper (written in ink; one side of the paper only)*
- *bibliography*
- *rough draft*

CHIEF JOSEPH

Your finished paper should show evidence of revision when compared to your rough draft. Double check for spelling and grammatical errors. Do not scratch out on your finished paper. If you make a mistake, rewrite it. Please note that this is a three-paragraph paper. Do not write two or four paragraphs. Look at your grade sheet to be sure that you meet the grading requirements.

© Good Apple GA-1672

Name _____ Date _____

Grade Sheet

Biographical Sketch

_____ Follows 3-paragraph format as outlined below (60 points):

      _____ 1st paragraph—introduction (20 of 60 points)

      _____ 2nd paragraph—personality/character (20 of 60 points)

      _____ 3rd paragraph—biography/famous works/importance (20 of 60 points)

_____ Student turned in these things (10 points):

      _____ rough draft (5 of 10 points)

      _____ bibliography (no encyclopedias) (5 of 10 points)

_____ Writing is grammatically correct. (10 points)

_____ Writing is free of spelling errors. (5 points)

_____ Good sentence structure and variety (5 points)

_____ Rough draft indicates revision process. (5 points)

_____ Paper is neat and presented in correct order. (5 points)

Total possible points 100   **Total points earned _____**

Comments:

_____
_____
_____
_____
_____
_____
_____

Teacher Instructions

Current Events Notebook

One of the major complaints that many teachers of social studies hear is that the subject matter isn't relevant. This is the perfect project to counter that complaint. It will also initiate some lively class discussions. Ideally, the current events notebook should be a year-long project, but you can always cut it to six, twelve, or eighteen weeks.

appropriate subjects for use: all social studies
critical thinking skills developed: knowledge, comprehension, analysis, synthesis, evaluation

Students should purchase a large spiral notebook. It will be used for this project only. Have them staple their instruction sheets (page 6) in the front of their notebooks.

Grading for this activity may be formal (use the formal grade sheet on page 7 for each article a student critiques) or informal (use page 8 and just put a check if students complete the critique). It is less time-consuming to use the informal grade sheet.

When using the informal grade sheet, the number of articles to be critiqued each week is up to you. A blank space for listing the number required is included on the student instruction sheet. Regardless of when students complete their articles, you can give them a grade at the end of 10 completed articles. Allow students the opportunity to share their articles with the class. The last 15 to 30 minutes of class on Friday work well.

Hint # 1: Place a cardboard box in the class. Students can deposit their notebooks in it on Friday after class. This makes it easy to keep up with the notebooks. (If you do it in more than one class, label each box.) Put the box in a safe place after the students leave.

Hint # 2: After 10 articles, assign a grade. (If you use the check system, 10 checks = 100.) Then staple the 10 articles together. This way, you don't have to flip through pages and pages to get to the most recent article.

Hint # 3: When sharing articles with the class, students should use their most current one. Obviously, only a few students can share their articles each week. Require the student to lead the class in a short discussion of the article. It's amazing what they learn from each other.

Name _____   Date _____

> **Student Instructions**

Current Events Notebook   Due Date: _____

A current events notebook is a wonderful way for you to learn about the many fascinating events that occur in your area, your state, your country, and around the world. For this assignment, you will be required to keep a current events notebook. The general goals for this assignment include the following:

1. To discover the relationship between past, present, and future
2. To foster a knowledge of world and regional affairs
3. To increase sensitivity to the diversity among people
4. To identify primary and secondary sources and their uses and limitations
5. To enhance oral and written communication skills
6. To clarify your own opinions
7. To differentiate between fact and opinion

Requirements

1. You must read and critique _____ article(s) a week. The article(s) should be current and should reflect and enhance the area or subject that we are studying.
2. Several students will be randomly selected to share and discuss their article(s) with the class. This will be on _____.
3. Notebooks should be turned in every _____.
4. Write neatly (in pen only) on the front of your paper.
5. Do not use the notebook for anything else.

Format for Critique

1. Source (see sample below)—Skip a line before going on.
2. Summary of article (*who, what, when, where, how*)
3. Examine and think about the problem or idea presented in the article. What is your response to the article? Why?
4. How is the event (or person) significant? Give reasons for your answers.
5. Tie your article to our current lessons.

Sample Source Citation

Byline (Assoc. Press or Author), "Title of Article", <u>Title of Newspaper</u>, Date, Section #, Page #.

Author of article. (Year). "Title of Article". <u>Magazine</u>, Vol. #, page #.

Name _____ Date _____

Grade Sheet

Current Events Notebook

Formal

Article # _____

_____ Source citation (20 points)

_____ Summary (20 points)

_____ Response to article (20 points)

_____ Significance of article (20 points)

_____ Relevance to our study (20 points)

Total possible points 100**Total points earned _____**

Comments:

_____
_____
_____
_____
_____
_____
_____
_____
_____
_____
_____
_____

Name _____ Date _____

Grade Sheet

Current Events Notebook

Informal

Articles completed satisfactorily and turned in on time:

_____ Article 1 (10 points)

_____ Article 2 (10 points)

_____ Article 3 (10 points)

_____ Article 4 (10 points)

_____ Article 5 (10 points)

_____ Article 6 (10 points)

_____ Article 7 (10 points)

_____ Article 8 (10 points)

_____ Article 9 (10 points)

_____ Article 10 (10 points)

Total possible points 100   **Total points earned _____**

Comments:

_____

_____

_____

_____

_____

_____

_____

_____

Teacher Instructions

Cookbook Project

appropriate subjects for use: world or regional geography, world history, anthropology, sociology

critical thinking skills developed: knowledge, comprehension, application, analysis, synthesis, evaluation

Be prepared for fun and laughter when you begin this project. Although it's a lot of work, students will enjoy doing it. You can assign it as a group or as an individual project. (No more than five students to a group.) Be sure to allow ample class time for students to use to work on the project.

The student or group of students will research and develop a cookbook. Each cookbook is to include five complete menus (a menu constituting one meal) from a country of the student's (s') choice, as well as an explanation of why the foods are popular in the chosen country. The goal of the project is to increase research skills, encourage creativity, foster cooperation, and develop an appreciation of ethnic groups and cultures.

Hint # 1: Assign a country to each student or group so that there is no excessive repetition.

Hint # 2: Most school libraries don't have enough sources for this project, so go to your local public library and check out cookbooks and travel books. Put a piece of masking tape on each book and number it. This way, you can keep track of your books.

Hint # 3: As a culmination of the project, have each student or group prepare a recipe from the newly-created cookbook. Designate a day for a "tasting party". Display the cookbooks at the party so the students can see and evaluate each other's work. Later, the students might share their cookbooks with another class.

Name _____ Date _____

Student Instructions

Cookbook Project

Due Date: _____

Creating a cookbook is the perfect way to learn all about a country and its most popular and delicious foods. Your country is _____.

Steps:

1. Read about your country. Begin research on foods from your country.

2. Gather an assortment of recipes. Don't forget the common drink. (Remember to look for patterns and representations of the culture. For example, perhaps the majority of people in the country do not eat pork. Be sure to relate foods to customs, climate, etc.)

3. Prepare a bibliography as you go. Index cards are a good way to keep up with this kind of information.

4. Start to formulate menus from the recipes. You must have five complete menus (one menu constituting one meal). Don't use a recipe more than once.

5. Organize your menus and recipes. Continue reading about the country.

6. Think of a title for your cookbook. Be creative!

7. Write the foreword of the cookbook which will explain the relationship between customs, climate, heritage, etc., and the foods. You may want to write a brief introduction for each menu, especially if the dishes are regional.

8. Illustrate/decorate the pages. Some of you may have access to a computer.

9. Make your table of contents.

10. Don't forget your bibliography. You must have a minimum of five sources. At least two of the sources must not be cookbooks. The bibliography should be the last page in the cookbook.

11. Compile your cookbook. Have fun! Be creative!

Name _____ Date _____

Grade Sheet

Cookbook Project

_____ Overall appearance is good. Project is clean, with no ragged edges. Writing/typing is neat and easy to read. (25 of 100 points)

_____ Visual reflects that a planning stage was utilized. Cookbook is presented in a logical, sequential manner. (25 of 100 points)

_____ Creativity is exhibited and used to enhance the finished product. (20 of 100 points)

_____ Followed criteria as described in handout (30 of 100 points)

      1. Appropriate sources included (10 of 30 points)

      2. At least five sources cited (10 of 30 points)

      3. Five menus, with no repetition of recipes, are featured. (10 of 30 points)

Total possible points 100   **Total points earned** _____

Comments:

_____
_____
_____
_____
_____
_____
_____
_____
_____
_____

Teacher Instructions

Careers Project

critical thinking skills developed: knowledge, comprehension, analysis, evaluation

This project provides students with the opportunity to explore various careers. It also helps them develop oral presentation skills since the projects are not written.

Copy and cut the careers sheet (page 13) into strips. You can add others if you think your students are interested in other particular careers. Give a strip to each student and have him or her record the career on his or her project sheet (page 14). Or, drop all the slips in a paper bag and have each student reach in and pick one. Students seem to enjoy this blind approach, but be ready for noise as they moan and/or laugh about their careers.

Students should use at least two sources for this project. Your school counselor and librarian should have books and other information on various careers. Encourage students to contact an actual person who performs their assigned jobs. Most people don't mind explaining their jobs to students.

Hint # 1: Students can use the yellow pages to locate a company who hires people for their assigned careers. Help them prepare a list of questions.

Hint # 2: Give students a minimum of two weeks to do all the necessary research. Encourage students to practice their presentations in front of a mirror before giving them in class.

Careers Sheet

Attorney	Furniture Salesman	Veterinarian
Car Mechanic	Model	Musician
Physician (general practice)	Life Insurance Salesman	College Professor
Home Health Aid	Actor/Actress	Tour Guide
Physician (specialty)	Stockbroker	Cosmetologist/Barber
Plumber	Medical Assistant	Electrician
Public School Teacher	Newspaper Reporter	Upholsterer
Architect	Librarian	Respiratory Therapist
Registered Nurse	Restaurant Manager	Carpenter
Welder	Brick Mason	Occupational Therapist
Licensed Practical Nurse	Social Worker	Zookeeper
Heavy Machine Operator	Electrical Engineer	Factory Worker
Computer Programmer	Physical Therapist	Marine Biologist
Construction Worker	Bank Teller	Travel Agent
Computer Operator	Occupational Therapist	Professional Wrestler
Psychologist	Banker	Day Care Operator
Small Appliance Repairperson	Secretary	Engineer
High School Coach	Graphic Artist	Author

Name _____   Date _____

Student Instructions

Careers Project

Due Date: _____

Choosing a career is a very important decision. Your career choice will have a profound impact on your whole life.

In this activity, you are to research and prepare an oral presentation on an assigned career. You are required to have at least two sources. If possible, contact someone who presently holds the job you've been assigned. Be sure to use current sources.

Your assigned occupation is _____.

Your oral presentation will be on _____.

You must discover the following information about your career:

1. training/educational requirements

2. certification/testing requirements

3. career options available

4. average first-year salary in our geographic region

5. expected salary per year in five years and within ten years

6. benefits that typically go with the job

7. job stability and prospects for the future

8. "typical" day (hours worked, etc.)

9. interesting information about your career

10. All of your sources of information (written bibliography) should be attached to your grade sheet.

Practice your presentation at home. Make eye contact with your audience. Be creative so that you don't bore the class.

Name _____ Date _____

Grade Sheet

Careers Project

Oral Presentation Grade Sheet

_____ (15 points) Included training, educational, testing requirements

_____ (15 points) Included career options/salary expectations

_____ (15 points) Included benefits, job stability, and future prospects

_____ (15 points) Included facts about typical day/interesting information

_____ (15 points) Bibliography included with appropriate sources

_____ (15 points) Used appropriate gestures (stood still, looked at audience, spoke clearly, etc.)

_____ (10 points) Displayed creativity

Total possible points 100   **Total points earned _____**

Comments:

_____
_____
_____
_____
_____
_____
_____
_____
_____
_____

Teacher Instructions

Country Scrapbook

When your students are studying different world regions, chances are you don't have time to cover each student's depth of knowledge about one country as well as increase his or her understanding of similarities within a cultural region.

appropriate subjects for use: world or regional geography, world history
critical thinking skills developed: knowledge, comprehension, application, analysis, synthesis, evaluation

A country scrapbook should be assigned at the beginning of a unit. Students should be able to contribute information based on their research to your class discussions. The project due date should fall near the culmination of the unit.

A project of this type can be assigned individually or as a group effort. This enables you to assist students having difficulty and encourage the use of appropriate sources. Travel books and cookbooks may be needed for this project. If your school library doesn't have these resources, go to the local public library and check some out. Put a piece of masking tape on each book and number it. This way, you can keep track of your books.

When assembling their scrapbooks, be sure to let students know that they can buy scrapbooks or photo albums to use, but some of the best scrapbooks can be made using two pieces of posterboard tied together, with sheets of paper in between. Construction paper also works very well.

Hint # 1: Assign each student a country to eliminate repetition.

Hint # 2: Do not allow students to photocopy maps, pictures, etc. All work should be original.

Hint # 3: As a culmination of the project, have each student prepare a recipe from a menu of the country he or she prepared. Designate a day for a "tasting party". Display the scrapbooks at the party. Later, the students might share their party with another class.

Hint # 4: During class discussions, have students note similarities and differences between their countries. This will increase critical thinking skills.

Name _____   Date _____

Student Instructions

Country Scrapbook

Due Date: _____

Creating a country scrapbook is a fun way to learn many fascinating things about a country. You are to research and prepare a scrapbook on the following country: _____.
You should include the following sections in your scrapbook:

1. Map of country
2. History
3. Type and organization of government
4. Brief biographical sketch(es) of main governmental officials (probably no more than 2 or 3)
5. Agriculture/Industry
6. Customs (including religion)
7. A menu representative of your country (one menu constituting a meal)
8. Three biographical sketches of famous people from your assigned country
9. Three famous landmarks
10. Bibliography (at least five sources, with only one encyclopedia)

Directions:

1. Begin your research. (Record your source. Note cards work well.)
2. Formalize/organize your research.
3. Decide on format and begin.
4. Organize your work. Be creative. Do not use photocopies.
5. Think of a title. Then develop a cover and title page.
6. Complete a table of contents.
7. Compile your scrapbook.

As you research your country and work on your scrapbook, think about the relationship of your country to our area of study. Consider the similarities in development, the physical and cultural geography of the country, and political and economic situations.

Name _____ Date _____

Grade Sheet

Country Scrapbook

_____ Map of country (10 points)

_____ History (10 points)

_____ Government/Government officials (20 points)

_____ Agriculture/Industry (15 points)

_____ Customs, including religion (15 points)

_____ Menu (10 points)

_____ Biographical sketches of famous people (30 points)

_____ Landmarks (30 points)

_____ Bibliography (25 points)

_____ Creativity/Neatness/Originality (35 points)

Total possible points 200   **Total points earned** _____

Grade = # of points _____ divided by 2 = _____

Comments:

_____
_____
_____
_____
_____
_____
_____
_____

Teacher Instructions

Position Paper

Students usually have opinions on almost any topic. The problem is that their opinions are often based on feeling instead of fact. Researching and defending a position on a topic is an excellent method for helping students develop educated opinions and make logical choices.

appropriate subjects for use: all social studies

critical thinking skills developed: knowledge, comprehension, application, analysis, synthesis, evaluation

In this activity, you will give students a topic statement. (Example: The United States government should/should not continue price supports to farmers.) Each student will then research the topic, form an opinion on the topic (based on research), and write a five-paragraph paper supporting and defending his or her position. Remind the students to be very careful of unsupported generalities. They should be looking for three facts that will justify their opinions. They are to argue the pros and cons in this paper.

Students' papers should have five paragraphs. The first paragraph should contain a statement of each student's position and a brief history of the topic. The second through fourth paragraphs should each contain one fact and a discussion of that fact. The fifth paragraph should be a conclusion which restates the position and the three facts.

Hint # 1: Don't assign "emotionally charged" topics. Students are more likely to use feeling instead of fact if the topic is one like school prayer or adoption. Ideally, pick something that they don't know much about.

Hint # 2: You might want to assign the first position paper as an in-class, group project. This will let you help students separate facts from feelings.

Hint # 3: Require at least three current sources. Students should include the *Reader's Guide to Periodical Literature* as one source.

Name _____ Date _____

Student Instructions

Position Paper

Due Date: _____

It is easy to have an opinion on a topic. However, many opinions are based on feelings instead of fact. In this activity, you will be researching and defending a position you take on a particular topic. The topic you will be researching is _____

_____.

Based on your research, you are to develop and defend your position on the topic. You will write a five-paragraph essay stating and defending your position. You are not to discuss the pros and cons, only your own position. The facts that you discuss should support your position.

The five paragraphs should consist of the following:

1st paragraph—statement of your position and a brief history of the topic

2nd paragraph—one fact and a discussion of the fact

3rd paragraph—second fact and a discussion of the fact

4th paragraph—third fact and a discussion of the fact

5th paragraph—conclusion, restatement of position and facts, no unsupported generalities

Papers should be double-spaced (if typed), written on one side of the paper, free of errors, and neat.

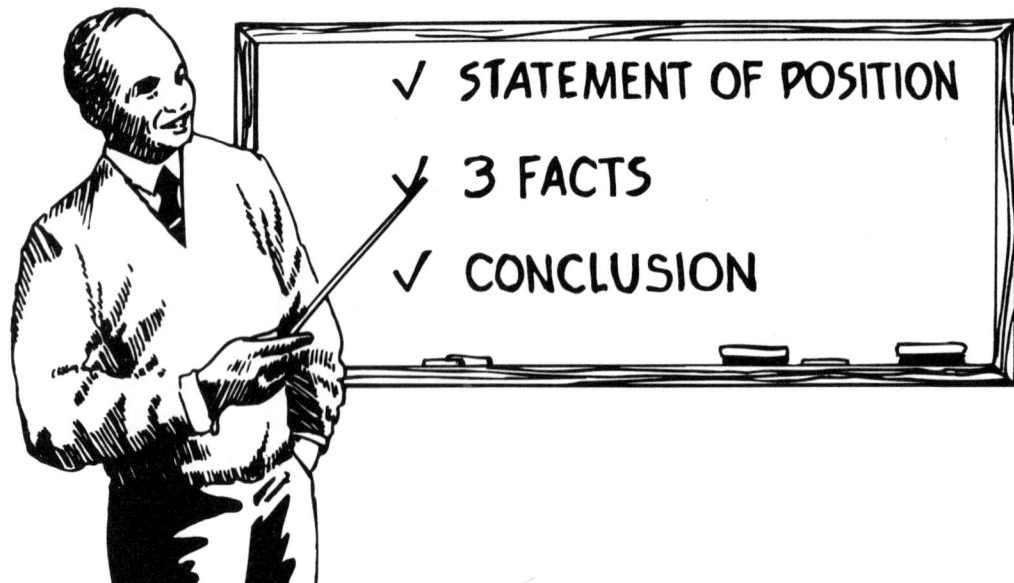

Name _____ Date _____

Grade Sheet

Position Paper

_____ (20 points) Introduction (statement of position, history)

_____ (10 points) 2nd paragraph (fact and discussion)

_____ (10 points) 3rd paragraph (fact and discussion)

_____ (10 points) 4th paragraph (fact and discussion)

_____ (20 points) Conclusion (no unsupported generalities, restatement of position and facts)

_____ (15 points) Bibliography

_____ (5 points) Grammar/Sentence structure

_____ (5 points) Spelling

_____ (5 points) Neatness

Total possible points 100   Total points earned _____

Comments:

_____
_____
_____
_____
_____
_____
_____
_____

Teacher Instructions

Create a Country

appropriate subjects for use: all social studies

critical thinking skills developed: knowledge, comprehension, application, analysis, synthesis, evaluation

This innovative project requires integrating skills and knowledge from all the social studies. The students must build upon their knowledge to create a "perfect" country. They will discover that utopia does not exist. As they make choices in one area, it limits choices in other areas. There are no right or wrong answers. The thinking and decision-making processes are the important parts of this project.

The project should be completed in scrapbook form. This can involve scrapbooks or photo albums purchased from a store, or students can make wonderful scrapbooks using posterboard, construction paper, staples, yarn, etc.

A project of this kind works well as a cooperative effort. The students must sort through their differences as they create their countries.

Hint: You can require students to share their countries with the class. This gives students the opportunity to explain and justify their choices.

Name _____ Date _____

Student Instructions

Create a Country

Due Date: _____

You are going to create the "perfect" country. You must make choices in regard to the government and the economics system. These choices will affect your other decisions, so be sure to think carefully.

Your finished product should be in scrapbook form. No table of contents is required, just be sure your order is logical.

You should include the following in your finished work:

1. Name of country
2. Location (include longitude and latitude)
3. Map
4. Type of government
5. Organization of government
6. Economic system (include role of government)
7. Main economic activities (relate to climate, resources, etc.)
8. Healthcare
9. Social welfare systems (How will you provide for the poor and elderly?)
10. Military
11. Taxation (How will you pay for the services provided?)

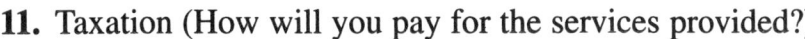

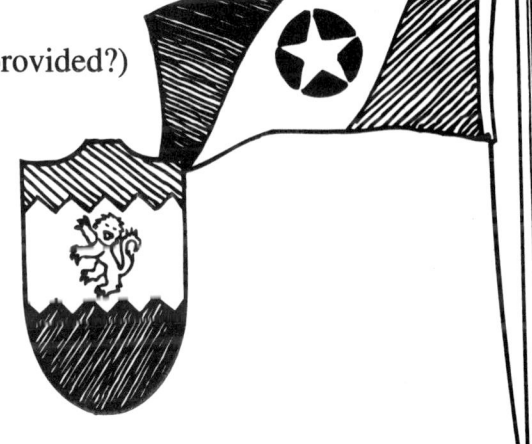

Name _____   Date _____

Grade Sheet

Create a Country

_____ (5 points) Location/map

_____ (15 points) Type/organization of government

_____ (15 points) Economics systems/economic activities

_____ (10 points) Healthcare

_____ (10 points) Social welfare system

_____ (10 points) Military

_____ (10 points) Taxation

_____ (5 points) Neatness/Originality

_____ (20 points) Choices show connection, are logical, and are presented coherently.

Total possible points 100   Total points earned _____

Comments:

_____

_____

_____

_____

_____

_____

_____

_____

_____

_____

Decades Project

appropriate subjects for use: all social studies

critical thinking skills developed: knowledge, comprehension, application, analysis, synthesis, evaluation

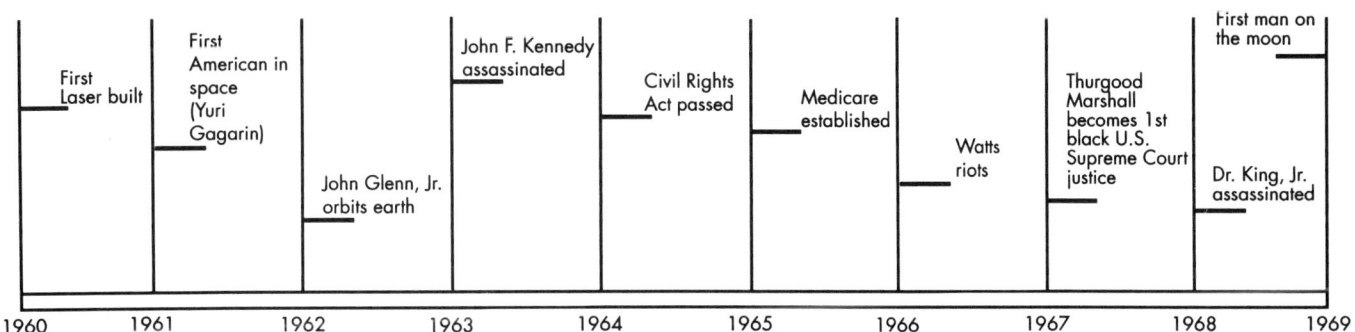

This project is designed to integrate and expand students' knowledge in U.S. and world history. It also requires the integration of information from other disciplines.

Divide your class into groups and assign each group a decade. (Example: 1960–1969) The groups are to research and prepare an oral and visual presentation on their assigned decades. The groups will be required to "teach" the class about their decades. Require the groups to use an entire class period for their presentations (minus 5 to 10 minutes for roll taking and set-up). This will force the students to dig for information if they know they must teach for 45 to 50 minutes.

Individual written reports can be required if you desire. Students should choose one area of research for their decades and prepare a written report. (Example: World events during the 1960s)

Hint # 1: The visuals can be displayed in the classroom or in the hallway. Make a sign identifying each decade and hang it above the visuals. (Students often appreciate having their work displayed. For those students who might do sloppy work, this might encourage them to be neater.)

Hint # 2: Allow students to critique each other at the end of all presentations. You would need to require students to make notes on each presentation.

Name _____ Date _____

Student Instructions

Decades Project
Due Date: _____

Group Presentation

A decade can be packed full of many fascinating and interesting events. In a group, you will be researching and preparing an oral and visual presentation on an assigned decade. You and your group will be expected to "teach" the class about the decade. The presentation should last _____ minutes. You are to include but are not limited to the following:

1. World events (wars, treaties, government changes, etc.)
2. U.S. events (political, economic, social, etc.)
3. Inventions/Inventors
4. Music/Arts/Literature
5. Pop culture (fads, lifestyles, etc.)
6. Disasters (natural and man-made)
7. Medical advances
8. Other (Be creative and think!)

Your group must develop and incorporate into your presentation several visual aids. The visuals should be attractive, neat, and suitable for display. They should also be large enough to see from a distance. You are to include but are not limited to the following:

1. Time line of significant events
2. Map (depicting location of significant events)
3. Pictorial display of the U.S. culture during your decade

One complete group bibliography should be handed in at the time of your oral presentation.

Your presentation should be given on _____.
(Be sure your group is ready.)

Individual Written Reports
Due Date: _____

Each group member is expected to choose one area of research related to the assigned decade and prepare a written report. You should focus on one of the topics and cover it comprehensively. (Example: Music/Arts/Literature of the 1960s)

The paper should be _____ pages in length, written in pen or typed, and double-spaced. Your individual bibliography should be attached and should include at least two sources. You will also be required to turn in your rough draft with revisions.

Name _____ Date _____

Grade Sheet

Decades Project

Oral Group Presentation

Research Skills (25 points)

_____ Efficient use of library and class time (15 of 25 points)

_____ Bibliography/Adequate sources (10 of 25 points)

Group Skills (10 points)

_____ Equal participation (5 of 10 points)

_____ Appropriate group behavior (5 of 10 points)

Group Delivery Skills (50 points)

_____ Well organized (flows) (10 of 50 points)

_____ Visual display (15 of 50 points)

_____ Creativity (10 of 50 points)

_____ Effectiveness of presentation (15 of 50 points)

Individual Delivery Skills (15 points)

_____ Organization/preparation (5 of 15 points)

_____ Used appropriate gestures (looked at audience, didn't sway or rock, etc.) (5 of 15 points)

_____ Effectiveness of presentation (5 of 15 points)

Total possible points 100   **Total points earned _____**

Comments:

_____
_____
_____
_____
_____

Name _____ Date _____

Grade Sheet

Decades Project

Individual Written Report Grading Sheet

_____ Contains an acceptable introduction (20 points)

_____ Body of paper is comprehensive. (20 points)

_____ Contains an acceptable conclusion (20 points)

_____ Writing is grammatically correct. (10 points)

_____ Good sentence structure and variety (5 points)

_____ Writing is free of spelling errors. (5 points)

_____ Student turned in the following: (20 points)

           _____ Rough draft with revisions (10 of 20 points)

           _____ Bibliography (at least 2 sources) (10 of 20 points)

Total possible points 100   **Total points earned** _____

Comments:

_____

_____

_____

_____

_____

_____

_____

_____

Teacher Instructions

Create a Game

If you are hunting for the perfect culminating activity to your year of instruction in social studies, this is it! Create a Game taps students' knowledge and requires them to apply

appropriate subjects for use: all social studies

critical thinking skills developed: knowledge, comprehension, application, analysis, synthesis, evaluation

that knowledge in a creative manner. It also provides valuable reinforcement to those lessons learned back in September and allows them to work cooperatively on a fun activity.

The objective is for students to develop a game (complete with instructions, playing pieces, and creative packaging) to review and test the material learned in your class. Once the games are finished, groups of students will play the other class members' games and complete an evaluation. You can assign a grade based on these evaluations by adding the total number of points using the key on the students' evaluations (page 31).

Hint # 1: Plan a day when students can brainstorm game ideas. Encourage students to think of original ways to develop a "commercial" game.

Hint # 2: Remind students to include more than "facts and figures" in their games. Thinking skills should also be incorporated.

Create a Game

Due Date: _____

Pretend you are an entrepreneur starting a new game company. Before you can get funding from the bank, you must create a fun, educational game covering what you've learned this year. Your game must meet the following criteria:

- Include clear, precise directions

- Must be made as much as possible and not bought

- Box that holds the game must be decorated and include the game's name.

- Creativity should be used to enhance game and game box.

- Game must be educational.

- All materials needed to play must be included.

- Game should be original or an original adaptation of a commercial game.

Name _____ Date _____

Evaluator(s): _____

Game Title: _____

Total Score: _____

Grade Sheet »»»

Create a Game

Student Evaluation of Game

Circle the number that corresponds with your perception of the game.

    1 stands for strongly disagree—5 stands for strongly agree

Directions are clear, precise, and easy to follow.

    1   2   3   4   5

Game is attractive, neat, and clean.

    1   2   3   4   5

The majority of the game is made, not bought.

    1   2   3   4   5

Game is educational.

    1   2   3   4   5

Creativity is displayed.

    1   2   3   4   5

Grade Key:	
5 =	20 points
4 =	15 points
3 =	10 points
2 =	5 points
1 =	0 points

Total possible points 100   **Total points earned** _____

Comments:

_____

_____

_____

_____

_____

_____

Culture Mobile

A mobile is a creative way for students to demonstrate their knowledge of a foreign country or culture. Students can illustrate different countries, or they can do all the same one, as each mobile will be unique. The project can be completed at school or at home and can be assigned at any point during the year.

appropriate subjects for use: world geography, world history, cultural studies

critical thinking skills developed: knowledge, comprehension, application, analysis, synthesis

Hint # 1: If you assign a country or a culture that you haven't studied, allow time for students to do research.

Hint # 2: Ask your media specialist to save old magazines that are no longer being circulated.

Hint # 3: Allow students to share their mobiles with the class before hanging them in the classroom or hallway for an interesting display.

Name _____   Date _____

Student Instructions

Culture Mobile

A culture mobile is a great way to learn all kinds of interesting things about another country or culture. Create your own by thinking about

Due Date: _____
Culture or Country: _____

things that make your assigned country or culture unique. Using old magazines, cut out 10 pictures that best represent different aspects of your country. Glue each picture onto its own piece of construction paper. Then cut out around the picture so that the construction paper forms a backing. Write several sentences on the back of each picture explaining why it is representative of the culture or country. Assemble your mobile using wooden dowels or a coat hanger. Remember to make it visually attractive. Be prepared to share your mobile with the class and explain your choices and how they are representative of your country or culture.

Materials needed:

- small wooden dowels or coat hangers
- yarn or string
- old magazines
- construction paper
- glue or rubber cement

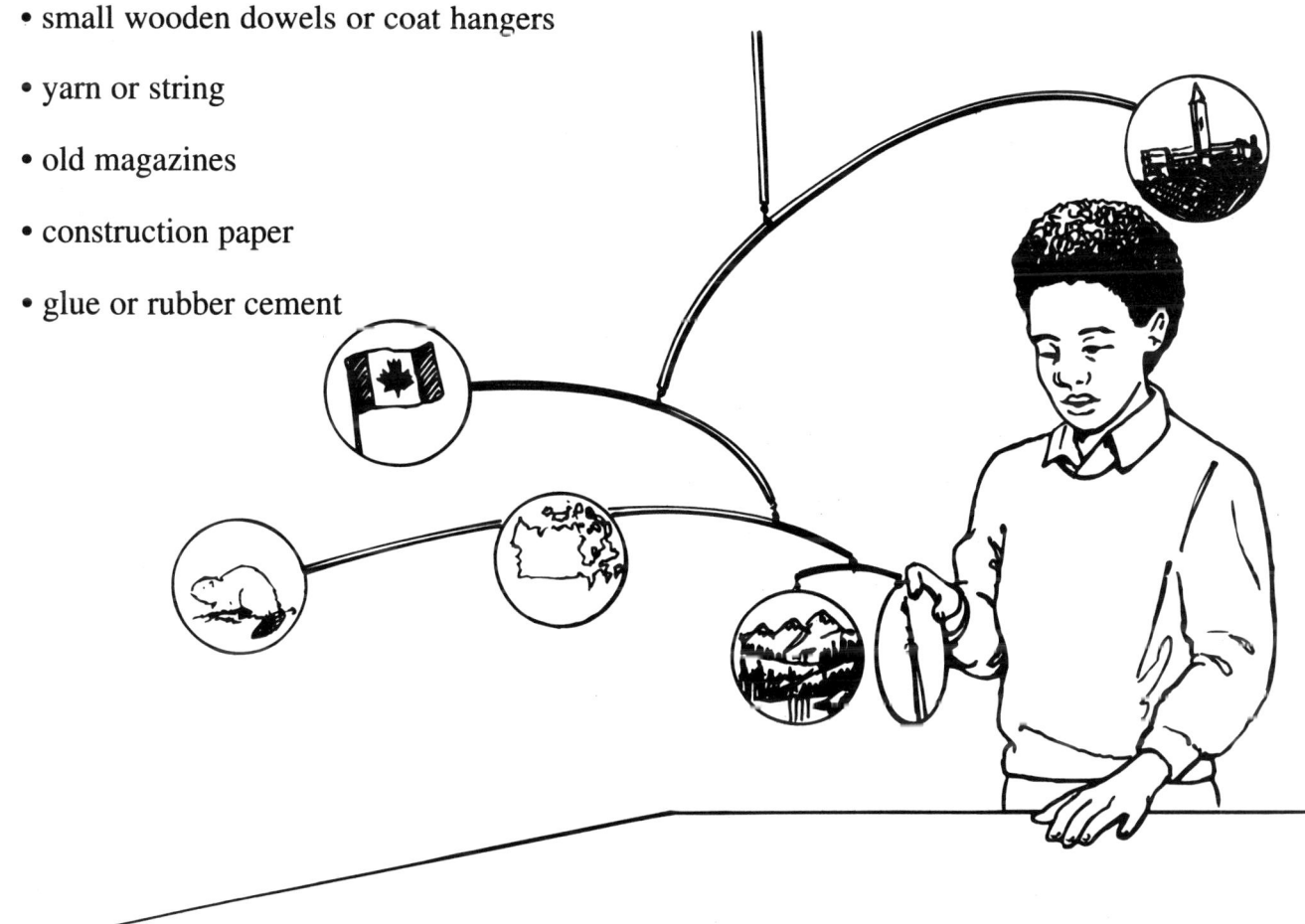

Name _____ Date _____

Grade Sheet

Culture Mobile

_____ Included 10 pictures (20 points)

_____ Provided an explanation on back of each picture (20 points)

_____ Pictures represent unique or important part of the culture. (20 points)

_____ Explanations are clear and meaningful. (20 points)

_____ Mobile is neat and attractive. (10 points)

_____ Planning stage was utilized during construction. (10 points)

Total possible points 100   **Total points earned** _____

Comments:

_____

_____

_____

_____

_____

_____

_____

_____

_____

_____

_____

_____

_____

Teacher Instructions

Government in Action

appropriate subjects for use: all social studies

critical thinking skills developed: knowledge, comprehension, application, analysis, synthesis, evaluation

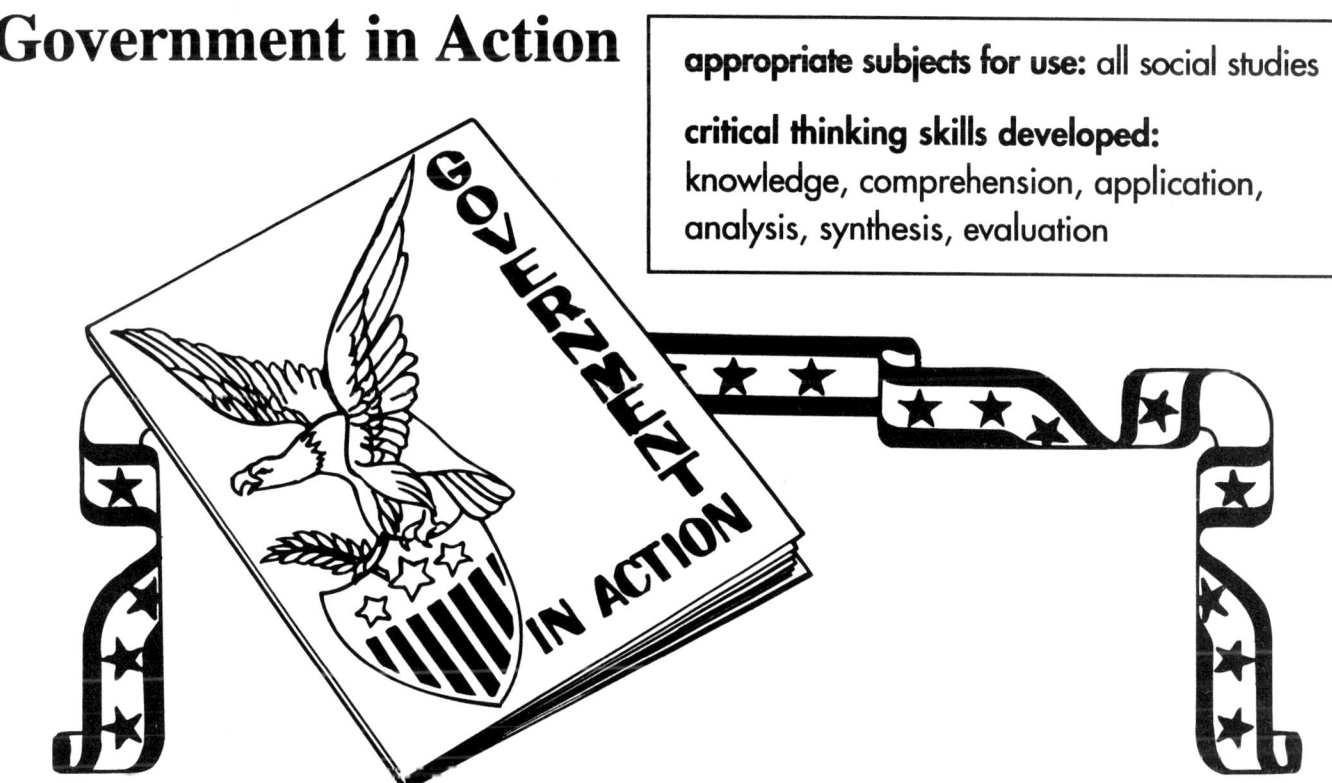

Civic education is becoming increasingly important not only in the United States, but worldwide. To increase your students' knowledge and understanding of how the United States government works, have them create a scrapbook illustrating the three branches of government. This project is the perfect complement to a unit on civics or U.S. history, but it will also work as a "stand alone" project. Students can work individually or in groups. However you choose to implement it, a better understanding of governmental operations should be the result.

The scrapbook should be broken into three sections: legislative, executive, and judicial. Each of the sections should include three newspaper articles that the student has critiqued, a political cartoon, and a letter to the editor.

Hint # 1: Save newspapers for several weeks. It's not necessary that all the articles be "hot off the press".

Hint # 2: If you are doing this as a "stand alone" project, plan for a day of instruction on the roles of the three branches of government.

Hint # 3: Teach your students how to do a source citation using the APA or MLA style book. Both should be available in your media center or public library.

Name _____ Date _____

Student Instructions

Government in Action

Due Date: _____

This project provides the perfect chance for you to discover for yourself some of the principles of the U.S. government, how our government operates, what others think of governmental practices, as well as what you think about them. You are to create a "branches of government" scrapbook containing three sections—legislative, executive, and judicial. Each of the sections should include the following:

- three newspaper articles about the branch—In each, write a source citation, summarize the article in three or four sentences, and then explain the significance of the article or how it illustrates governmental operations. Also include your own analysis.

- a political cartoon about some aspect of the branch and your analysis of what the cartoon means and why (If you can't find one, draw one and explain it.)

- a letter to the editor about a governmental action and your response (If you can't find one, write one yourself.)

Assemble this information in scrapbook form with an appropriate title. Your scrapbook can be bought or made. The scrapbook should be creative, organized, and neat. If you have access to a computer, use it. But most of all, enjoy learning as you plan and implement this project.

© Good Apple GA-1672

Name _____ Date _____

Grade Sheet

Government in Action

Legislative Branch

_____ 3 articles with analysis (15 points)

_____ 1 political cartoon with analysis (5 points)

_____ 1 letter to the editor with analysis (5 points)

_____ Writing is clear, concise, and demonstrates understanding. (5 points)

Executive Branch

_____ 3 articles with analysis (15 points)

_____ 1 political cartoon with analysis (5 points)

_____ 1 letter to the editor with analysis (5 points)

_____ Writing is clear, concise, and demonstrates understanding. (5 points)

Judicial Branch

_____ 3 articles with analysis (15 points)

_____ 1 political cartoon with analysis (5 points)

_____ 1 letter to the editor with analysis (5 points)

_____ Writing is clear, concise, and demonstrates understanding. (5 points)

_____ Scrapbook is attractive, neat, and reflects utilization of a planning stage. (5 points)

_____ Appropriate choices in selection of articles (5 points)

Total possible points 100   **Total points earned** _____

Comments:

_____

_____

_____

_____

_____

Teacher Instructions

History Alive!

appropriate subjects for use: all social studies

critical thinking skills developed: knowledge, comprehension, application, analysis, synthesis, evaluation

Some of the best books are based on stories that have been told to younger generations. Help your students discover the richness of history with this project.

Tell students to select a family member or friend who has witnessed a historical event. After they have identified a person and an event, they should research the historical time period and interview the person. Based on the research and interview, students are to write a short story using descriptive and narrative techniques.

Hint # 1: Plan class time to help students write interview questions. Discuss interviewing techniques with them.

Hint # 2: Remind students that the historical event doesn't have to be dramatic. Most people have a vivid memory or reaction to an event in history. The point is to help them view history as more than textbook facts. History is also personal experiences and reactions.

Hint # 3: Allow time for students to share their stories with the class. Choose some or all of the stories to share with younger students, too.

Name _____   Date _____

Student Instructions

History Alive!

Due Date: _____

Historical fiction is valuable because it helps history come alive. You are to do what writers do and bring history to life. Choose a friend or acquaintance who has witnessed a historical event or vividly remembers the event. From an interview with this person and research on the historical time frame, you will write a short story that brings history to life.

Directions:

1. Choose a person to interview based on earlier stories you have heard. If you have difficulty selecting a person, remember that history comes in many forms. Talk to your friends and relatives. You may be surprised at their recollections.

2. Once you have selected your subject and the time period, it is time to prepare for the interview by doing research. Research the time period or event that you are going to explore. This will allow you to ask specific questions. Remember that your interviewee may have a different point of view than the one taken in news accounts or history books, but your research will give you both points of view.

3. Set up a time to interview the person. Before your interview, prepare a list of questions. Remember to focus on the "local color" which will help you set the scene when you write your short story. Also ask for specific details, especially details that may not have made the news. You also want to find out the impact of the event on the person's life. Write down your questions and leave plenty of room to record the answers. You might also consider using a tape recorder.

4. After your interview, choose the most interesting quotes, reactions, and facts from your notes. At this point, you may need to go back to the library for more information. You might also need to call the person to clarify a point. Don't forget to thank the person you interviewed with a note or a telephone call.

5. Create a story based on the interview and research. Make your writing vivid by including details and making the characters real.

6. Proofread, revise, and edit your writing before writing or typing the final draft.

Name _____   Date _____

Grade Sheet

History Alive!

_____ Historical background is interwoven throughout story. (25 points)

_____ Story has a beginning, middle, and end. (20 points)

_____ Characters are portrayed realistically. (15 points)

_____ Writing is vivid and interesting, including the use of dialogue. (20 points)

_____ Writing is grammatically correct. (10 points)

_____ Spelling is correct. (10 points)

Total possible points 100   Total points earned _____

Comments:

_____
_____
_____
_____
_____
_____
_____
_____
_____
_____
_____
_____
_____

Teacher Instructions

Parade of History

Whether you are studying the United States, ancient cultures, or your own state, there are many people who have made significant contributions to history. Make history come alive for your students as they increase their breadth and depth of knowledge.

appropriate subjects for use: world or regional geography, world history, state history

critical thinking skills developed: knowledge, comprehension, synthesis

Have each student choose and research the life of an important historical figure and the time period during which he or she lived. Students should get your approval but not share the name of their historical figure with their classmates. They will prepare a brief presentation pretending to be their chosen persons (speaking in first person) and create costumes to dress as the historical figures might have dressed.

Hint # 1: Encourage students to choose interesting facts so that the other students will remember the information. You might set up a time to meet briefly with each student to discuss his or her progress and presentation.

Hint # 2: Costumes can be created from clothing and items found around the home. Props can be made from cardboard and construction paper.

Hint # 3: Remind students that they should rehearse their presentations at home so that they can deliver them without notes.

Name _____ Date _____

Student Instructions

Parade of History

Choose a historical figure and research his or her life and the historical time period during which he or she lived. Based on your research, list at least 25 facts. Then choose 10 to 15 of the most interesting facts and prepare a presentation you will give pretending you are the historical person. For example: "I was born before the Civil War in a log cabin . . ." Conclude your presentation with "My name is _____." You should also research the dress of the time and recreate a period costume so that you can dress as your character for the presentation.

Historical figure: _____

Time period during which historical figure lived: _____

Date of Presentation: _____

As you plan your presentation, choose the most important and interesting facts about your historical figure. Practice your presentation at home so that you can deliver it without having to look at notes. Remember that you ARE that person, if only for a few minutes. When you plan your costume, look around your house for items that can be used. Don't forget that you can create hats and other items out of construction paper.

Grade Sheet

Name _____ Date _____

_____ Sufficient and appropriate choice of information (25 points)

_____ Costume reflects time period and person. (25 points)

_____ Delivery is clear, interesting, and easy-to-follow. (25 points)

_____ Good public speaking skills displayed, including posture and eye contact (25 points)

Total possible points 100   **Total points earned** _____

Comments:

_____

_____

_____

_____

_____

Photo Field Trip

appropriate subjects for use: all social studies

critical thinking skills developed: knowledge, comprehension, application, analysis, synthesis, evaluation

Field trips offer students a chance to experience history and geography firsthand. Naturally, prior to the field trip, you will have studied about the place you are visiting and the historical time frame. To help students process information and extend learning once you have returned to the classroom, turn an "ordinary" field trip into a photo opportunity.

Students will photograph important and interesting sites and features. They should also record information about the sites that they photograph. Upon return, students can have the pictures developed and create albums featuring the field trip, complete with pictures and captions, narratives about their experiences on the trip, and evaluations of the importance of the site they visited and how it ties in to the curriculum.

Hint # 1: If possible, purchase disposable cameras for each student. You can add the cost to the field trip fee.

Hint # 2: Encourage students to get some shots of themselves as they explore the site. This personalizes their visit. Another student can take the picture.

Hint # 3: Students don't have to purchase photo albums or scrapbooks. They can make their own out of cardboard and construction paper.

Hint # 4: When you schedule the field trip, make sure that photography is allowed.

Name _____ Date _____

Student Instructions

Photo Field Trip

Due Date: _____

On our field trip to _____, you are to become a photographer as you explore the site. You are to photograph interesting and important places during the field trip. Record information and write a description about each site that you photograph so that when your film is developed, you can explain why you took the photograph. Ask another student to take a picture (with your camera) that includes you in it. This will personalize the trip even more. Keep in mind that you want to try not to shoot pictures directly into the sun.

When we return from the trip, you should have your pictures developed. These pictures will form the basis of a photo scrapbook. In the scrapbook, be sure to include the following:

- a label and caption on each photograph

- a one- to two-page narrative about your experiences on the field trip including

    1. fun information,

    2. an analysis of the importance of the place(s) visited in relation to history,

    3. an explanation of how the trip helped contribute to your understanding of your school lessons, including specific examples.

All of this should be organized in a logical sequence in your photo scrapbook. The scrapbook can be made out of cardboard and construction paper.

Name _____ Date _____

Grade Sheet

Photo Field Trip

_____ Included an appropriate caption for each picture with an analysis of the importance of the site (30 points)

_____ Narrative is interesting and informative. (20 points)

_____ Narrative explained how the field trip contributed to an overall understanding of studies. (30 points)

_____ Correct grammar and spelling on captions and narrative (10 points)

_____ Photo scrapbook is neat and attractive. (10 points)

Total possible points 100   **Total points earned** _____

Comments:

Teacher Instructions

Student Teacher

appropriate subjects for use: all social studies

critical thinking skills developed: knowledge, comprehension, application, analysis, synthesis, evaluation

Being a teacher, you know that you really learn about a subject as you prepare to teach the information. Give your students the same opportunity while varying the classroom instructional technique.

Assign each student a topic or heading from a textbook. Have each student plan a lesson and prepare to teach the class. Each student should also prepare several multiple choice questions that you can use to make a quiz.

Hint # 1: Plan a day to take students to the media center so that they can learn and present more than just textbook material.

Hint # 2: This is a wonderful activity when you sense that student interest is lagging.

Hint # 3: After all students have had a chance to be "the teacher", ask them each to write a paragraph on their experience as a teacher. They should include an evaluation of their presentation.

Name _____ Date _____

Student Instructions

Student Teacher

Due Date: _____

Here is your chance to be the teacher. That's right, you are going to teach the class. But before you can, you must do what every good teacher does—prepare.

You are to prepare a lesson on _____ and plan to teach the class on _____. You are allowed to use notes, but don't read to the class. Good teachers know their subject and can tell about it in interesting ways. You should also develop a visual aid. This can be a poster, a model, pictures, or anything that you can use to make your teaching "come alive". Remember that you are the teacher. Your class members expect you to be the expert, so be prepared to answer questions.

Name _____ Date _____

Topic or page numbers: _____

Grade Sheet

Student Teacher

_____ Assignment complete and ready on due date (10 points)

_____ Personal interpretation of material by the student (10 points)

_____ Thorough coverage of material (10 points)

_____ Exhibited factual knowledge of topic (10 points)

_____ Responded knowledgeably to questions (10 points)

_____ Used a visual to enhance presentation (10 points)

_____ Good public speaking skills displayed (10 points)

_____ Student taught instead of reading the material. (10 points)

_____ Student turned in multiple choice questions. (10 points)

_____ Student wrote evaluation of the experience. (10 points)

Total possible points 100   **Total points earned** _____

Comments:

_____
_____
_____
_____
_____
_____
_____
_____
_____